ONE
LITTLE
MOUSE

ONE LITTLE MOUSE

by Dori Chaconas

illustrated by LeUyen Pham

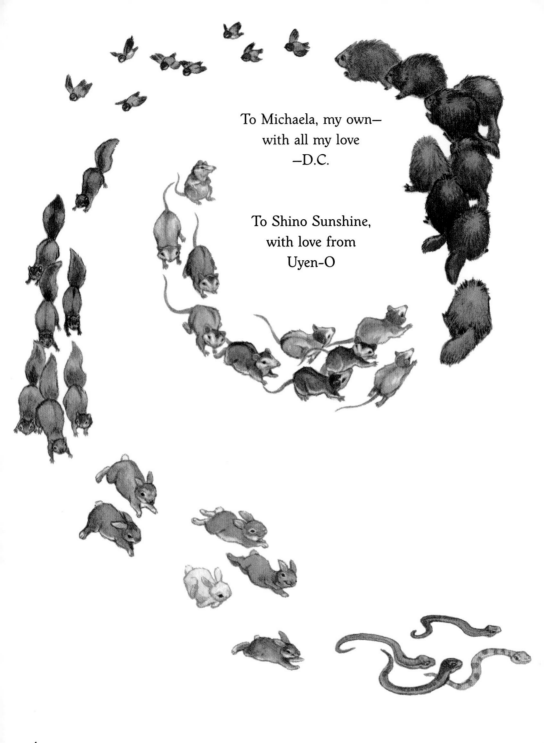

To Michaela, my own—
with all my love
—D.C.

To Shino Sunshine,
with love from
Uyen-O

This edition is reprinted by arrangement with Viking, a division of Penguin Putnam Books
for Young Readers. All Rights Reserved.

Little Book version of *One Little Mouse* published by Scott Foresman.

ISBN: 0-328-19167-1

18   18

One little mouse took a look at his house
Deep in the woodland ground.
"This nest is too small! Not roomy at all!
There must be a new one around."

Two blackish moles peeked out of their holes
And called to the mouse passing by,
"We have a fine nest in which you can rest."
So little Mouse thought he would try.

But their diet was wormish,
And that made Mouse squirmish.
He very soon said, "Good-bye."

Three meadow frogs were leaping from logs.
"You'll like sleeping here," they said.
Mouse thanked them politely, but curling up tightly
He found it too cold for a bed.

With a wheeze and a sneeze,
He was sure he would freeze.
"This never will do!" he said.

Four bobwhite quail ran up from the vale.
"If you're looking for someplace to rest,
We have a nice hollow, and if you will follow,
We think we have room for a guest."

But Mouse found it bumpy
And clumpy and lumpy,
Just too many eggs in the nest!

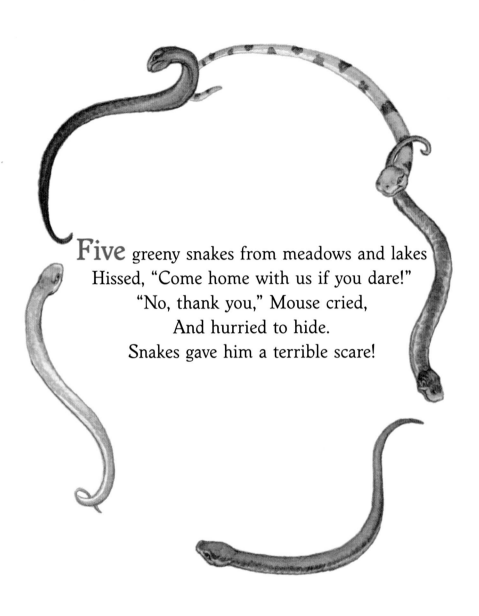

Five greeny snakes from meadows and lakes
Hissed, "Come home with us if you dare!"
"No, thank you," Mouse cried,
And hurried to hide.
Snakes gave him a terrible scare!

Six baby cottontails hopped along hilly trails.
"Come, little Mouse, share our bed."
"Oh thank you," said Mouse. "I'm in need of a house."
And he happily laid down his head.

But the cottontails bunched up
And crunched up and hunched up.
"And soon I'll be scrunched up!" Mouse said.

Seven gray squirrels
Ran in circles and swirls,
Then carried Mouse up to their nest.
"You may stay here with us
If you don't make a fuss."
And Mouse said, "I will do my best."

But the nut nest was clicky
And clacky and cracky.
He left without one bit of rest.

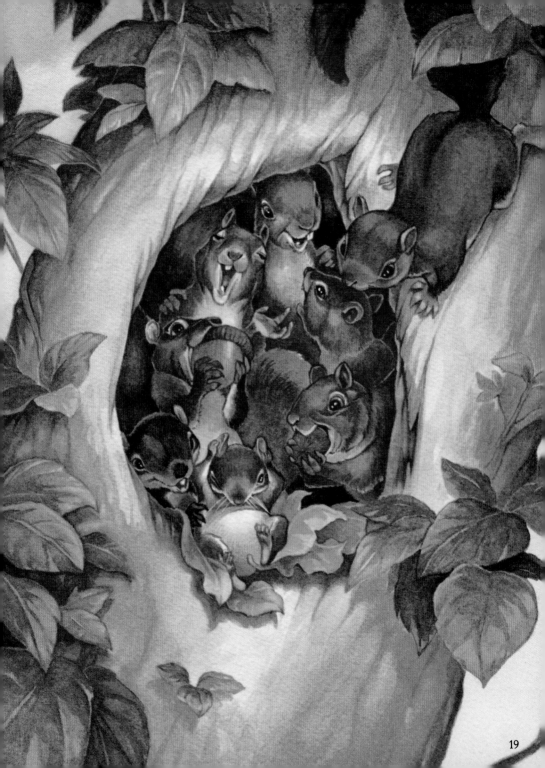

Eight chickadees flew in with the breeze.
"We have a fine place in the willow."
But Mouse said, "Dear me! I can't sleep in a tree!
Imagine a branch for a pillow!"

Nine porcupine waddled by in a line.
They called to the mouse, "Good day!
We have a nice den, right here in the glen."
"Thank you," Mouse answered. "I'll stay."

But their sharp quills were sticking
And picking and pricking.
So Mouse quickly went on his way.

Ten small opossums were eating plum blossoms.
"Come on, sleep with us," they were singing.
They knotted his tail, and Mouse let out a wail
To find himself suddenly swinging.

"A terrible tizzy! I'm upside-down dizzy!
A mouse tail is not made for clinging."

Then Mouse turned around to the darkening wood
And scampered along just as fast as he could,
Back to his own little comfortable house
(So tiny and tidy, just right for a mouse),
And when evening shadows crept over the ground
And covered the woodland, here's what was found:

Ten small opossums asleep in the glen.
Nine porcupine nestled up in their den.
Eight chickadees roosting
High in the willows.
Seven gray squirrels using
Soft tails for pillows.

Six baby cottontails snug in their nest.
Five greeny snakes coiled up for a rest.
Four bobwhite quail very still in the vale.
Three meadow frogs sleeping on logs.
Two blackish moles deep in their holes.

And one little mouse,
One tired little mouse,
One content little mouse,
Sound asleep in his house.